Am I Not Your Sin

The cover art was created by artist Kim Soojin. She assembled the layers or fragments of memories in the poetry collection from old newspapers in a collage. Titled "People Trying to Become Birds," the artwork measures 18.5 centimeters in width and 13 centimeters in height.

Two sheets of paper are overlapped for the cover. The halftone outer page features a dark pink hue, reminiscent of the sky at dusk and evokes the low voice of someone who has long departed. A subtle scent of grass lingers around the cover.

The center of the cover page is cut out in the shape of two birds, revealing a second layer of paper underneath. The underlying paper is a blue-tinted news photo, showing the entangled legs of standing and fallen individuals. The image exudes a sense of unease, tension, and fear, mingled with the smell of blood and sweat.

Of the two birds on the cover, the one on the top seems to be looking down, while the one on the bottom seems to be soaring upward. The two birds are almost touching. A diagonal line crossing the cover page from the top left corner to the bottom right resembles a tree branch, delicately held in the beak of the bird on top. The tails of the two birds are connected by a thin, bent line.

In the top right corner of the cover, the words "Am I Not Your Sin" are inscribed in white.

Below it, in smaller white letters, are two lines: "A collection of new poems by Choi Ji-In," and "Translated by Stella Kim." The logos for "K-poet" and the publisher "Asia" adorn the bottom left of the cover.

This brief description provides an explanation of the cover design for the audiobook or the Braille editions of this poetry collection.

AM I NOT YOUR SIN

Choi Ji-In

Contents

AM I NOT YOUR SIN

The southeasterly wind comes, but not my love
who promised to come
I sit, but my love does not come; I lie down,
but sleep does not come
Both sleep and my love are lost; everything in
between, I have lost.

This "Farmer's Song" (Deullorae) was recorded in the village of Inji in the town of Jisang, Jindo County, South Jeolla Province, on June 22, 1965.

Curve

The past says, Do something, anything, to avoid ruin; I sat on a chair, mulling over life.

Several incidents; Jeju, Okinawa, Taipei, Manila, Singapore, Sri Lanka, Madagascar, Haiti, Hokkaido

Sand grains on the beach
They are similar sentiments, anticipating that the future has been interrupted, but to a place that those moving forward do not know,

Because there is nothing that I can do other than to write
I stand
a citizen facing a barricade

because I am lonely

When a colleague was found out and dragged off by the police, I sat crouched in a chair, hiding my small body

Something like fireworks exploded in the sky Dimmed fragments Crumbled brick walls The smell of gunpowder assailed my nostrils

One day you vanished
never
to come back Alone
I was left in the city
What is in the sealed box?

It feels as though
spectators would be waiting behind the door
I want to rest,
thought the pea. Motionless
underground
it fathomed its fate

*

Born in the same year as the child who would not sin, I enjoyed a relatively peaceful life Walking through his motherland; the streets that shout "Death to the dictator" I could see the dead vividly

Compared to him, I shouldn't have been born Therefore I will do what I can I will plan for later

Be enraged

For years

I have been reading a friend's posthumous poetry book

You said you wanted to be a tree in your next life

Wasn't enough I

doubt you know

how much I love you

It wouldn't be strange to cry

When I am no longer me

When you are no longer you

With my bare hands
I washed the dishes clean

In the summer, each house would open their windows and
become the wind to

Unknowable hearts would become transparent

I finished knitting the winter sweater
Now
It is vivid

The future says,

A Coniferous Tree

A white serpent-turned-tree lived for a thousand years

Numerous supports propping it up

Please live You can't crumble

Because I have to live

Covered things

I can barely remember your face

Being alive and being dead

Transparent numbers Stones

Standing at a fork in the road

You laughed, didn't you?

Like a lightning

Your face cracks

Like a lightning

the war images are transmitted throughout the world

Lonely, lofty, desolate

A photograph of the dead and the soon-to-be-dead, together, smiling

How many centuries will it take for a wounded soul to heal?

Lying on the floor on my stomach

I put the fallen leaves in the container They will blacken in the city

An order to kill an unarmed civilian

I knew that I would survive, along with people who have aged, like an object

A living deer keeps by a dead deer on the street.

Murmuring of the Night

Is the city lonesome?
I look down from the rooftop
Two people are walking side by side A shadow follows
lengthening and shortening
shortening and lengthening
End and the beginning I
can revolutionize Now
what should I do?
The red light comes on
The train runs through the platform
What lies before my eyes
East Asia from 1937 to 1947, when my grandfather lived; parted with friends at the the hospital and guzzled down hard liquor On the train

My long fingers
flip through ten years of solitude page by page
Aiming a gun at the enemy
Obeying the orders
alive
because I was alive
inheritance left to me
Saddled with debt for nearly all my life my family calculates the monthly sum we have to pay back If you hate me as I hate you
I feel like I've become someone wrong
Waking in the middle of the night you pull on the deep sunken silence O transparent and crystal-clear civilization
Guerrillas lying in ambush
From among the bushes

a dog jumps out

with a bone in its mouth

Under the dogwood in full bloom of the dead

I motion slowly, in an endless dream I hold my ground I must not forget you

Murmuring of the night

Perpetually running train

Missed opportunities and

the calm weather

Day and Night

1

Verily, verily, I say unto you

What becomes bare
helplessly

To love means
to live out

When everything was a mess

2

You used to be mischievous
You paid them back for your suffering
No, even more

Remember how I said I wanted to die because of you?
You probably forgot If you etch
all that in mind
how could you live

3

Please help
Sleep eludes me in the evening

An emergency vehicle
enters
the underground parking lot of an apartment complex

4

It resembled a frog Its body inflating and deflating We Ribbit Ribbit locked our bodies and inhaled

Breath

That there is nothing to rush

That rushing only leads to regret

If we stop

a moment

The earth of day and night tells stories

5

Those who remain
must do their part

Thankfully
both of them sank

It's fun
being with you
I would have been miserable had I been
squatting down alone

Because I am cold and lonely
For the last time

Holding

Breath

Too beautiful
What I've left behind

Darling
I cannot be rich
When am I not sad?
When you play on a slide

Giggle giggle
Giggle giggle

A bird
sits on a dead person

6

How nice would it be if our lives had answers?

Why do I wish that there were no answers?

Hope to shake off the past

and meet again someday

7

February 24, 2022

Russia attacked Ukraine

A war began

8

During the spring when seeds are sown

summer when those seeds grow
and autumn when the ripened crops are harvested
we were often miserable We
waited for the winter to come
In tranquil winter
we do not take walks and
stay home In those days
our hearts are calm

Thank goodness you were born

9

Those that make us feel
ugly, foolish,

inadequate,
and hopeless

Unite
In solidarity
If not, you will be plundered
and dominated
by those who consider you prey

Health
Food
Basic Income
Shelter
Education
We say to the warship
Get lost!

*

Pirate radio – what the Empire wants is not peace for foreign countries but for the people of its vassal states to fight to the death to weaken the enemy... There is no single morality... Why Joseon in the battlefield between the Qing and Japan... There is a man who fell asleep leaving his rifle unattended in the field... A bleeding man...

0
The one who answers questions
how did he arrive at those answers?
Without shame

Later we will
be stubborn old men

The radio frequency
reached a tree

There was a time when the crematorium
was packed full of corpses

I do not live in the house I built.

"After All, We Are" by Kim Soojin, collage newspaper image on canvas, left 728×605mm, 2018, right 500×600mm, 2019.

Scenery

The number of the dead
Feels indifferent
Inside and outside
A long line of cars at the checkpoint A jet liner
ready to take off A free man freely crossing
borders
Children
taken hostage are in the military truck
What signifies the outside
What is that outside the outside of?
They say everything grows well where people
are buried We used to play with empty shells
we dug out from the ground Spoons made with
melted duds are very hard
Where did all the birds go
Why does anger move down

Why do humans
stand at the bottom

Birds*

Liberation

Siphoned images

The time I haven't lived

Many Russians object to the war As the people have in the past

hopefully in this life

A ninety-year-old grandmother sits in a wooden chair

Driving a car to the meeting place, we talked about our future The interest rate is soaring

Over ten skeletal remains were found in the cave

Brothers divided the land among themselves and parted around three in the afternoon

This family is done

According to the testimony of a survivor, the

dead engulfed in flames twisted their bodies as though they'd come alive

The unspoken

No trespassing

A long tunnel

Several centuries have passed

Occasional lulls

I filled the shopping cart with clothes I liked My thoughts kept going

Humans do to humans

Images to be shattered

What has been scribbled on the corner of last year, lying on the beach and reading a book, and the year before that What I'd believed to be perfect

Unbeknownst

feeling indifferent

I called out your name

* Pau Casals i Defilló, "El cant dels ocells", live performance, UN Day Concert, General Assembly Hall, New York, October 24, 1971. "I haven't played in public for nearly forty years- I have to play today. This piece is called 'The song of the Birds.' The birds, in the sky, in the space, sing: Peace, peace, peace. The music is a music that Bach, Beethoven and all the greats would have admired and loved, and it is also the soul of my country: Catalonia."

Mole

Mourning the time I'd let slip away

Who said it The foundation is crumbling

Humans should move like migratory birds

Excesses, energies that roam the earth

Thunder clapped as the loudspeaker reached the end of silence

In the past you had a dream Swarming ants Uncontrollable heart

Am I not your sin

The words "I understand" resemble the back of the leaver

Amplitude

People who hid for weeks in the basement
storage under the crumbling grocery store
Spring without water and electricity and more
The family who buried the mother
Well,
prolonged war and
people unable to leave

A time
youth
sell possibilities
only to gain impossibility

The infinity is strange
What is big is too big and
what is small is too small

Vaccines acquired by major countries are being disposed of
The climate crisis
Heated asphalt
Hey there
What are you looking for

Boy, save me
This is a thankless job

Can live differently
Perhaps
To the extent where it can't get any worse
in different parts of the streets

A landslide buried the village

The end of growth
Labor is legally exploited

A bluegill flopping on the dirt floor
The face of a compassionate god
Jam-packed Naebu Expressway

Why do the dead not leave?

The city is being submerged

in a heavy fog
flickering
emergency light

Why should a human surmount nature

Father in his prime sits leaning against a pile of hay in his combat uniform Dead before I was born

Beautiful
because it has passed

Grandfather survived a close combat

I hope you miss me

Things I wrote standing
like an ancient tree

Dirty, shameful, and
honest

future I want

Look behind you
How far we've come

The End of Growth

The Lamb of the earth carrying sins of the world
There are things more plentiful in heaven and earth than what humans can imagine

The concentration of carbon dioxide
Rising sea level
Ocean acidification
Plastics and contaminants
Endangered and threatened species facing extinction
Melting glaciers
Expanding deserts
Intensifying storms
Other legacies
Divided and occupied regions

A world turned upside down

Foretelling the future

Nature and pretas (hungry ghosts) of the Nectar Ritual Painting

The throat is as narrow as the ear of a needle

but the gut towers over like Mount Taishan

Bared body

Vastly empty

Bad Woods

Another country
Another city
Another life's possibility

On an overpass
hung a banner one afternoon*
The lost one broke silence
and stuttering
chose his words

Concerning the brilliantly shining
and the pitch black
Concerning my me
Contemptible me
and the economy

We need dignity
not lies
Red letters on white background
*We don't want blockade, we want freedom

One running on the tracks
Running and running
until he disappeared

The remains of the day
The remains of the night
Under the care of the day
Under the care of the night

With eyes raised
Opening the mouth

and closing it
There is no form in beauty

Among the people, you are
a food court worker rubbing her eyes
Several tables

Even when sleeping, you answer me when I call
you

We gnaw away at each other's misfortune
My name is First Snow
The beginning and the end of fate
Dolls molded from clay
Pieces broken before placed in the kiln
The inside was completely empty

On a rainy day
I went by the back road
and threw them out in the field
All that passed
Everything

A youth**
fell from a tall building
to not kill in the battlefield

**I made this choice to object to this hell of a world. I hope you remember that I love you.

Do you believe there is room for change?
What about hope?
Everyone knows this world has gone wrong

There is no gas
Cars passed by
In a humming aquarium

you worked ‘til early morning and fell asleep
Love, the river is freezing over
It is too cold

Why am I a continual loop
Unable to answer anything properly

Everyone is alive
and because they were alive
they shook a sleeping man’s shoulders
and asked,

Are you alive?

Took a walk around an old cemetery
How many fears hold us captive?
Isn't it interesting?
That people used to live here.
A tiger mosquito gnawed at my ankle.

I love your rhythm
Is that the heart?

The Final Stop

You are incomprehensible the entire time I traverse the city

I am a load of whites, a load of blacks, a glue spot

The one-room basement studio where a family of three began has been torn down

What changed was not the world but me

I can't tell which way the train is running

Even in dreams

you can fall asleep and you can dream

A decade has passed The next decade and the decade after that have turned deathly pale

A cracked bowl and a street turning back

The shame of being alive

I cannot bear it

Past the field

Words precede and words precede

the end of the tunnel You correct your posture because your shoulders ache

What has passed are contained in a box

But when you open the box, there is nothing

A Quiet Affair

Face

Is pale

What is it?

Pressing firmly

Between thumb and forefinger

Brushed down arms

Till the coldness subsided

Distorted

Face

People of a neighborhood

to be demolished making kimchi

A tiled wall marked with the date of demolition

A god's teeth mark

Red lacquer

Residing here

Protruding rebars
Rebars Bulging

Wandering around the creek
Chasing after money and fame
But never amounting to anything

Where are you going?
Oh you who have survived

Do not say we are equal
in the face of death

Prohibit the prohibition

Before the storm

sweeps everything away

*

A twenty-six-year-old laborer was pulled into a shredder. Long ago his father had his hand stuck in a sawmill pulverizer.

*

A throat is cut

Throat

Throats

A browned bouquet of chrysanthemums

*

A cargo truck keeps on crossing the yellow line
Inside
What is happening
Before flipped
We are
Captivated by what?
Flowers
Through ice
The containers are stacked

Why can't I put myself down
How can I put my everyday life down

After a dreamy time

I am now back to my everyday life

I send half of my earnings home My father has to go to the hospital three times a week

Knock knock
Can I come in?

Wet shoes
A frog croaks
with every step

Under the tree
I take shelter from rain
Oh friend I
have no home to return to

The pit where people are buried
is like the pupil of the eye

In the Streets

If sound could illuminate the darkness
An empty space
revealed through death
There are many more deaths
to us, yet undiscovered
Half of my soul came from
the dead
Thump
Falling
Night
I am an old thought

Sowing

Heavy rain poured
Exposed the roots
at the edge of the field
Traces
of a pit where
people were lined up
and shot

*

(The address where the incident occurred and the remains were buried)

San39, Dupo-ri, Papyeong-myeon, Paju-si, Gyeonggi-do

This is the site where abducted anti-Communists

and civilians were massacred and buried during the Korean War in 1950. Please be careful not to cause any damage.

*

I dare ask
about life

How could I know life
when I do not know death

*

You were born under the Japanese rule and witnessed Korea's liberation

And shortly after, you went to fight for the war.

You suffered a gunshot wound on your left hand
but it created no problem on your life.

The soldiers of the Blue Dragon Division,
where I served, had violently killed
unarmed civilians in the Vietnam War.

I lay on my stomach in the fire lane and fired.
The gunshot and the kickback of the rifle
against my cheek.
A missed bullet is embedded in the dirt wall.

When grandmother dies,

she will be buried at the National Cemetery.
Her husband's remains in the family burial grounds
will be exhumed and buried with her.

October Fog

May God's mercy and blessings be with you

I refuse to be your servant,
even if I turn into a handful of ashes
in an unquenchable fire

On the streets,
beaten by batons,
enveloped in tear gas

burning city

*

On the day I longed for the departed,
I bit down on stones,

silent and still

How futile and vain
is the notion of foreseeing the world

We drink fake beer
when we speak of love
to avoid getting intoxicated

You should work less, son,
and write more

It's an all-too-obvious
soap opera-like affair

Sweltering heat and

the fallen migrant worker

More previous
than life

A stadium
Cheering people

*

For the sake of all humanity,
gathered together,
as many as there are

Take a good look, all of this means
that I love you

One day, a thousand years ago
I think I fell asleep like this

You squatted down in the veranda
and silently watched
your parents
making love
on a wooden chair
Never in their dreams did they imagine
Had they known, they would have realized
early on that you had changed

*

Father

My father...

What happened to you, I wonder
Your soul is escaping

The factory in Uijeongbu went up in flames
When you were young and I was a child we
used to spend time riding bicycles
in the empty lot

Before it turned into a pile of ashes

My pride My joy
You are no longer with me

We are only crossing from death to death

There is no way to stop

The relentless effort to cough up
the death lodged in the throat

Father
My father...

*

The belief that only those who believe
in deepening can be deepened

To love
those that have never loved before,
So that it doesn't become vain

The things we willingly forgot
Leaving your voice behind

Shoes
lined up side by side

Paju

When I'd nodded with a sad face
And the sunlight and silence
The day before yesterday feels like a long time ago
There will be times of joy and times of sorrow
In a small room veiled by black curtains
I fell asleep and fell asleep again Crossed the passage of time
I was sick for some time
On a day I reached the summit along the ridge
Weaving sleep and more sleep
By the forsythias in full bloom
Like a burnt forest
And the buildings of a distant city, the words left by those who departed from this world
Like a flock of lost migratory birds

with affection

with affection

I straightened my posture

Outlook

A worker bee wanders among artificial flowers.

When he was merely twenty years old, my uncle inhaled carbon monoxide and died.

A year ago my grandfather was hit by a car and killed.

My father stopped drinking for some time after he was diagnosed with cataracts. Asleep in the hospital ward, he murmured. That he was sorry. All my life I've apologized for everything. I sat by my father's side and covered one eye.

Sitting at the beach and watching the long-extended bridge, I was lost in thought. Momentary joy and old sorrow undulated in the waves.

We cannot return to the past.

An old woman cares for an even older woman. While my aunt was gone, my grandmother bumped her forehead. There was blood and a bump. Why did this happen precisely when I wasn't home? My aunt cried and went to the mountain, leaving my grandmother in care of the family.

Mother, have some rice cakes. Tomorrow is Chuseok.

A wild boar unearthed the graves in the family

burial grounds. My grandfather said he did not want to go into fire in death. We made a temporary grave, and he lived for a little longer. On the way I picked some mushrooms, washed them clean, and dried them on a wicker tray.

Removing
the rust on an iron plate

We sat round in the courtyard, eating and drinking until it grew dark. Somewhere along the way, without my mother and my father, alone I wandered through the residential area. Is this the only way to live and die? Such is life, said the night. There was a bitter taste in my mouth.

The young married couple took their three-year-old to the zoo. The child stood, holding the fence. The pictures from that day show all empty cages. A man in a maroon corduroy pants is watching the child.

Time passed and I forgot everything.

Mom ate burnt rice.

The kernels of corn that were planted last spring are strewn on the floor of the greenhouse.

Daydream

This is a heavy snowstorm.
It is the first space show in two hundred years.
The skyscraper in the distance is this nation's pride.
The passersby were badly injured by a steel pipe that fell from the construction site, but
it ended as a simple accident.

Mr. Kim from Jeju met a storm and
drifted on the sea
for nine days and nights. The sea swallowed others
and he alone reached the eastern coast of Annam (Vietnam). There he
married and had six children. For forty years
he lived

and reached the western coast of Jeju alone
Ten or so years later
he passed away at the age of eighty-seven.
That was several years ago.

I worked at a glass bottle factory,
picking out defects. Imperialists and traitors resemble each other.
Ever since I was young, I used to look at the world map.

Redemption comes from odd places.

Feeling dazed
two, three months passed.

The big river flows East,
one small misstep, and you can't escape despair.

I've been waiting for you, welcome.

Excuse me?
With widened eyes
I looked at you.

A New World

We cannot know what life is or what it means to be human. We reach death without knowing anything. So we must break through the unknown with ignorance.

The Proposal

The day and night have been switched
While you sleep, I am wide-eyed

Swiftly passing judgments—thinking you were very flawed—I tried to comfort you but

I grew afraid once again
Afraid of growing poor and losing everything
If I didn't work
If I couldn't work

Trampling at work for several months
The feeling of being trampled and the well-lit living room
The sound of snores

A little later, the ailing you will go to work
and return home when it's dark
Soon after, you will fall asleep

Where did you go?
I seem to be very far

The river on the other side is frozen as if the waves are surging

I ask for forgiveness, please
May you not be defeated by misfortune

The flames swallow Mount Taishan
You glug, glug,
glug down water

Soldiers armed with swords and shields surround the enemy's stronghold

A struggle between myself and what is not me
Things I must write again

War and massacre
Innocent civilians who will be the first to be massacred

Very stubborn, I hear
That's bad for success, I hear

The world must love us
The ghost comes and goes several times a day

Everything comes in due time,
I say, feigning innocence

I will make a gold mask
Just for you
I promise

Several Incidents

1

Is it aimed at the head

What does my face look like

2

Oh, my love, how harsh you are in this cruel world

Let us go

to the north

Love in the streets, amid the raining bullets

you

My lucid grandmother sat in front of the ancestral rites table

and prayed

for our souls to not lose their way

If you didn't die and lived for a long time
and wrote the next then
you would've borrowed the enemy's writing style

The North Vietnamese poet who had condemned Lyndon Johnson as a "war lunatic" has
risen from his grave and
is wandering through the jungle

My once blossoming youth is naturally aging
Come
to the South
There was no time for sorrow

during his and my father's time
How different survival and living are

If one starves for long
he might harm someone

I long for the yesterday that I haven't lived

3

Both my father and mother grew up without a father.
They were poor and were often
called bastards.
They fell in love.
My father barely managed to finish school

and when he went to work at construction sites, my mother
would stay home alone and
sometimes go see the ocean.
Sitting atop a seawall
she held on to her swelling belly.
She had to save money. I was
born in the year the Gulf War
broke out. They say many people died
and lost their homes. The war was aired live
via satellite.
Tanks crossing through the town,
soldiers passing through the desert, and
the AH-64 Apache helicopters. It was much later that
my laid-off father shouted at me to get him

a bottle of Toad soju. And much later than that
I recalled that summer and looked into the life that man stole from me and the life that had been stolen from him. Where was my mother at the time? Why didn't I look for my mother who didn't come back?
An iron top spins round and round,
boring a hole in the linoleum floor. Why is the past me
grieving? Why do the days of the past feel like
a made-up story?

4

The poet said,
Now I know, what poetry is

He wrote poetry all his life
In eternity
In the eternity of eternities

A serpent carries the world on its head
In its body
grows a tree
In a thousand years
In a thousand years of a thousand years

There was
nothing good or bad
nothing to believe in
I was your countless mistakes
The birds already knew Early on
they'd left and were gone

5

The Western forces surrounding Russia promised support for Ukraine but constantly changed their words
The leaders of each country proposed division under the guise of peace

People in trouble
People whose troubles have been ignored

I do not know
what war is like

While someone is dying
I am looking for a way to live

Strands of hair grow carelessly
O you
who are weak
like me

Dissolved families

On days I get wasted
I recall the face of my grandfather whom I have never seen in person
His picture on the wall looks down at his blood relation and

Blast
Once more
Blast!

Toward the rays of light pouring
from the sky

Loudly the dead dog barked

6

By what luck were we humans born into this world?

Asking for bones, asking for flesh, I was born into this world

Should I go here, should I go there, I came here looking for you

The way to the underworld is distant they say,
but outside is the nether world

7

Last night the wind blasted

I read aloud a paragraph from the new novel you wrote sitting against a wall. Don't stop. Once you cross this bridge, it's a new neighborhood. I promised myself not to hold back any longer. You are white as snow. And your hand brushes down my shoulder

Sawdust from the apple tree

smells like apples.

The time on the clock on the wall is wrong.

POET'S NOTE

1

If I have literary talent, it was given me by chance. I would like to share this life I have received for free with the people of the neighborhood I live in. I would like to read them aloud together for a long, long time.

2

Premiered in Art Jamsil, "Hana-ui yeonju-wa yeoreo gae-ui jungsim (One Performance and Several Centers)" is a poetry reading performance with music. Together with cellist Park SongA, I had the privilege of taking the stage multiple times. The drafts of my six poems intersected with Bach's Cello Suites, and led me to this moment. The entire time I worked on putting together this poetry collection, I could hear the cello music in my ears.

3

I would like to send my heart to Hwa Soo, my first reader and my love.

We have vowed never to give up on life and love. We will mourn when we feel sad; we will celebrate when we are joyful; and in this way, we will live out each other.

June 2023

Choi Ji-In

A CONVERSATION WITH THE POET

We Soared Together and Plummeted Together

Yang Juan (Essayist)

As I began this conversation with poet Choi Ji-In, there were several factors that I had to take into account. First, I acknowledged that I do not have the ability to analyze a poetry collection. Second, I recognized that my personal affection for him as a friend could very well bias my objective gaze. Lastly, I understood the importance of familiarizing myself with his first poetry collection *Naneun byeoge butteo jatta* (I Slept Against the Wall, Minumsa, 2017), which was published before we became acquainted, in order to explore the various sides of him that I were unknown to me. Choi Ji-In describes publishing a book as "tying the knot (wrapping up) of a period," which meant that it wouldn't be sufficient to merely read his latest poetry collection and ask him questions. Your own thoughts may have evolved from when you first began till now, but it is impossible to erase the time that has passed. This thought led me to the conclusion that I should make my confessions before we began our conversation:

1. I intend to approach his poetry collection guided by my emotions and intuition rather than trying to provide poetic analysis and insights.
2. Recognizing the challenges of turning off one's affection for another, I choose to let go of the hold on maintaining absolute objectivity.
3. I will not try to explain Choi Ji-In's entire life through the few years I have spent by his side.
4. I want to emphasize that this conversation

begins and ends with my perspective, as the one asking the questions.

As I headed to Paju Book City via Jayu-ro Motorway, I noticed trees lined up on both sides of the road. Since Choi Ji-In and I began to share a workspace together, we often drove along this road. Within a space spanning a mere 16 square meters, we would sit and engage in discussions about various topics Some ideas resonated between us, while others sparked clashes. And the words we shared during these conversations found their way into each other's works, taking on diverse forms an expressions.

*

I've noticed that you often take words from your surroundings and turn them into your own in your work. It is as if you always carry a big notebook around, ready to jot down useful phrases and sentences.

At some point after deciding to be a writer, I developed a habit of writing things down. Everyday language is something that has become an innate part of your being. Language that goes beyond conscious thought. In literature, particularly in poetry, I believe that narratability holds significant importance—stories that are shared from mouth to mouth. Human existence predates the invention of written scripts. We developed scripts and tried to document everything but failed. The majority of modern poetry is composed of written letters, but before they were written, they were spoken. They were sounds. I write down everyday language because I believe that there are many more poems made up of spoken words than written letters. In this sense, reading poetry aloud is an extremely important way to read poetry. There is a profound emotional connection that envelops the reader when written words pass through the reader's body and become sounds.

*

In Choi Ji-In's first poetry collection *Naneun byeoge butteo jatta* (I Slept Against the Wall) is a period of time in his life that I was unaware of. The poems in the collection were generally dark. I sensed that he was capturing raw reality with keenly honed phrases. The world depicted in this collection was characterized by "countless walls," a place without "any room for rest" ("Contract Working"). He tries to sleep against one of those walls.

His second poetry collection *Ilhago ilhago sarang-eul hago* (Working and Working and Making Love, Changbi, 2022) includes a period of time during which I had the opportunity to know him. Ji-In confesses, "I grow afraid when I speak of love/I know it will destroy me." But he begins with a resolute declaration: "In the distance, I see the islands/Now I will cross the sea" ("Islands"). It leads me to wonder whether the words he encounters in his surroundings, which he then recreates, are typically ones with sharp edges that were hurled at him and became lodged in his body.

*

I remember a conversation we had about our initial resolutions., where we contemplated the notion that it might be even more daunting to admit that our original resolve remains unchanged. When ones has tied a knot, concluding a period of his life, it is natural for their thoughts and perspectives to evolve as they enter the next phase. Is there anything that you perceive to have changed within yourself from the time of your first poetry collection to the second poetry collection?

It is difficult to notice changes, even the smallest ones, in the process. Only after some time has passed that there come moments when I suddenly find my past self unfamiliar. Instances when what I once deemed important appears trivial, or what I once considered trivial now feels important; moments when I sense a gap between the before and the after. It is illogical to talk about what has changed and what I may have missed because I do not fully know myself. All I can do is ask.

I grapple with a kind of compulsion, thinking that as an artist, I should constantly strive for something new. The paradox lies in the fact that I have to make similar efforts to what I had been making before, in order to create something new. You have to keep on reading and writing. You have to face blank pieces of paper, and you have to be different from before. Where does distinction come from? I believe it stems from difference.

In the end, it was possible for me to create variations because the past version of myself has lived through those previous experiences.

There is a distinct atmosphere that feels more pronounced in this poetry collection compared to your previous ones. The direction of the verses seems clearer. You seemed to have focused particularly on wars and massacres. It seems as though your gaze naturally gravitated to the period that has been overshadowed by significant historical events. And I thought that this may have been the reason behind your decision to include the "Farmer's Song" (Deullorae), recorded in the village of Inji in the town of Jisang, Jindo County,

South Jeolla Province, on June 22, 1965.

The Japan-Korea Treaty was an extension of the Treaty of San Francisco. It further solidified the dominance of "empires." I believe that literary imagination sprouts from the earth. I want to write with unwavering dedication, much like a farmer who tends to the land, cultivating and sowing seeds.

Wars and massacres are old stories in human history. It is often said that memories permeate spaces. In this sense, the memories stored within the human body are passed down to the next generation. The Pacific War and the Korean War that our grandparents' generation witnessed; the Vietnam War and the Soviet-Afghan War that our parents' generation witnessed; and the Gulf War, the War in Afghanistan, and the Russia-Ukraine War that our generation has witnessed... I believe that there are memories of the subconscious that are shared across three generations, and even across the three generations of those generations. To revive these memories, I thought that it is necessary to remove the yokes of ideology and lend our ears to the voices of the people.

*

The poetry collection *Am I Not Your Sin* encompasses a period of Choi Ji-In's life that I have had the privilege of witnessing up close. He told me that there is a history of massacre in Paju, where our workspace is located. The entire time he was compiling this poetry collection, he shared stories about wars and massacres with me. Each time these discussions came to an end, a profound sense of helplessness settled upon me. Alongside these weighty topics, which we could not do anything about, we engaged in discussions on seemingly trivial yet meaningful matters, such as the type of home we wanted to live in or the type of car we wanted to drive. We didn't have much time to dwell in a state of helplessness. The monthly rent for our workspace, as well as utility bills and money for food, compelled us to get up and work.

*

I thought the incidents explored in this poetry collection encompassed our past, present, and future. Some people strive to become variations on their journey toward the future, but others are denied the opportunity to even embrace that possibility. In your latest poetry collection, I sense a contradictions It is not brazen enough to turn a blind eye to tragedies, yet it is not courageous enough to become a variation on its path toward the future. I'm curious to understand how you see these contradictions now, as you have studied and poetically expressed these incidents in your poetry collection.

I find an increasing number of contradictory desires in myself, to the extent where it becomes difficult to distinguish between my desires and those imposed by the world. What is it that we genuinely seek? Can true equality and peace be achieved by humanity? Inequality and unpeace must be the very first human deficiencies. The stories that originate from metadiscourses ultimately end up, once again, in the realm of everyday life. I am just one person, grappling with the constant struggle to avoid collapsing.

Among the poems in the collection, my personal favorite is the first poem, "Curve." It depicts a human who can do nothing "other than to write" faced with several brutal incidents. Moving beyond anger and regret, he arrives at a scene where "with [his] bare hands/[he] washed the dishes clean." This transformation reminded me of a curveball in baseball—a pitch that rises high, and then suddenly dives to the lowest point. I saw a reflection of myself in this portrayal. I often find myself becoming enraged about certain incidents, but eventually I forget and move on. The first poem appeared to foreshadow the ending, perhaps a rather nihilistic one. Yet you still chose to compile these poems into a book. It seems you have tied a knot, concluding a period of your life, because you believed that doing so was significant in itself.

While I was working on this poetry collection, I had collections of works by poets Kim Su-yeong, Shin Dong-yup, and Yi Yongak by my side, along with other brilliant works by contemporary poets.

The true meaning of poetry emerges when the poet and the readers come together. The meaning always follows the work. And it changes over time and in different spaces. Can my literature bear "meaning"? I have a feeling that this collection will serve as some kind of a turning point for me.

Even if our lives may come to a futile end, we cannot stop asking questions.

*

While he was working on his latest poetry collection *Am I Not Your Sin*, I frequently observed Choi grappling with limitations. It seemed that he was struggling to digest significant events and translate them into his own words. During that time, he was also faced with some of the most important decisions of his life. We often discussed the massacres perpetrated in Vietnam and the war in Ukraine, but these topics often slipped down our list of priorities. The "days of the past" felt like "a made-up story," and while "someone [was] dying, I [was] looking for a way to live" ("An Incident"). What he was faced with was the limitation of guilt.

*

While reading *Am I Not Your Sin*, I had such an intense feeling about guilt and its limitations. While guilt has the power to stop me for a moment, it couldn't change the direction of my life. It forced me to face my weakness. Considering this, I am curious about how you feel now after finishing your book.

I'm scared.
What would the future look like?
What would you and I look like?

*

Last winter, the two of us went to a convenience store past midnight.

Eating isn't allowed inside. You can go outside and eat.

We took our cup noodles and sausages outside the building and had our dinner in the streets. Ji-In remarked, "I would've been miserable had I been... alone" ("Day and Night"). We laugh every time we talk about that night. Embarrassing events can become decent memories when you have someone to share them with.

As I read *Am I Not Your Sin*, I couldn't help but feel ashamed. Everything—both the things I had been oblivious to and the things I knew but chose to ignore—was laid bare for all to see. Had I been alone, I would have bottled up the shame I felt inside, but I found the strength to gather my courage and write down our conversation. It was okay because I wasn't alone. "Thank goodness you were born" ("Day and Night").

COMMENTARY

Living Out a World of Bad Infinity

Ko Myeong-cheol

(Literary critic, professor at Kwangwoon University)

1.

Here, in the face of the unspeakable horrors committed under colonial rule of empires that took place in "Jeju, Okinawa, Taipei, Manila, Singapore, Sri Lanka, Madagascar, Haiti, Hokkaido" and in the world of bad infinity where the socio-political context of the abovementioned horrors and civilized violence are entangled, stands a "citizen facing the barricades" "because there is nothing that [he] can do other than to write/[he stands]/because [he is] lonely" ("Curve"). This honest and succinct self-awareness of poet Choi Ji-In highlights the political and ethical challenges and the content format of his aesthetic practice that he must contemplate with intensity in a world of bad infinity, where atrocities that should not be silenced were committed under the guise of civilization or absolute goodness in places like Asia and Africa. Throughout his poetry, a prevailing sentiment of desolation emerges with exceptional significance. As he confronts the enemies against whom he harbors hostility behind the barricades, one might wonder, Shouldn't the poet foster anger that would fuel the determination for struggle rather than succumbing to desolation? In fact, this dualistic contradiction that both entwines and coerces these emotions to the same extent it pushes each other out dwells in the depths of this poetry collection, generating a unique poetic responsiveness from the poet who bravely stands on the frontlines of the struggle, while squarely facing the world of bad infinity.

2.

The war images are transmitted throughout the world

Lonely, lofty, desolate

A photograph of the dead and the soon-to-be-dead, together, smiling

How many centuries will it take for a wounded soul to heal?

— Excerpt from "A Coniferous Tree"

When did it all begin? With the United States-led Gulf War against Iraq in 1990, the world has watched the spectacle of state-of-the-art missile attacks and fighter jet bombings, reminiscent of scenes from war movies, transmitted through various mass media channels. It is no longer uncommon to witness and share conflicts and wars happening around the world in real-time. Thee "war images...transmitted throughout the world" have become a mere component shaping our complex everyday life on Earth. Nevertheless, the poet feels pain in the narrative of joy and sorrow, life and death, encapsulated in the "photograph of the dead and the soon-to-be-dead, together, smiling"—the "wounded soul." Do we truly understand why wars must occur? Can we comprehend why we are unable to do anything as we face the loss of countless lives, consumed by the extreme fear of death, in wars? Even if trite, fragmented, and foolish answers to these questions are scattered into the abyss, the poet forges his anger, blended with a "lonely, lofty, desolate" sentiment, through his sensitivity to poetic resistance against the bad infinity of the modern era.

3.

At this point, it is necessary to focus on Choi Ji-In's sensitivity to poetic resistance. In the poem "Several Incidents," there is a section where the first-person speaker reveals his painful past. This particular section captivates my attention. For Choi, the world of bad infinity, symbolized by war, is not a disconnected simulation of the spectacle of a war, detached from the mundane fabric of everyday life. It is not a mere reproduction of some grand and extraordinary sociopolitical conflicts in the history of the earth, offering an alternative spectacle within the monotonous daily routines. Instead, the war on the other side of the world overlaps entirely with the speaker's everyday life. Born in the "year the Gulf War broke out," the speaker is pushed to the brink of extreme poverty, ultimately leading to the disintegration of his family. From what we can infer, the speaker, born in 1990 around the outbreak of the Gulf War, saw his parents make desperate efforts to make ends meet by any means necessary. However, akin to the harrowing experiences witnessed during the Gulf War, where civilians endured immense sacrifices under the US-led military force, it is likely that the speaker's family fell into ruin from enduring sacrifices in all aspects of society, including the economy under the International Monetary Fund. But it is precisely within this ruin that the reader can encounter Choi's unique sensitivity as poetic resistance.

An iron top spins round and round,
boring a hole in the linoleum floor. Why is the past me
grieving? Why do the days of the past feel like
a made-up story?

— Excerpt from "Several Incidents"

For the first-person poetic speaker, the spinning top that "spins round and round/boring a hole in the linoleum floor" represents a poignant symbol of his parents' class reality—a world of impoverishment that seems nearly impossible to escape. It also signifies the unyielding and inescapable social structure, with its thick, towering barriers that appear insurmountable. In this context, the speaker internalizes a sense of shame, recognizing that an individual's relentless passion and ceaseless efforts alone cannot conquer this reality and social constrains of life. Consequently, the speaker's profound sadness instinctively manifests as an inward desire for all of these histories to be perceived not as realities but as illusions, a longing to be content in such an unrealistic perception. While this yearning may be criticized for evading reality, paradoxically, it is precisely because of this evasion that the anger directed at everything is inherently linked to the poet's profound sorrow. In other words, the poet's sensitivity is a mix of nihilistic desolation and sorrow of self-destruction, related to the burial ground of "images to be shattered" where "humans do to humans" ("Birds*") "many more deaths/...yet undiscovered" ("In the Streets") in the Gulf War, the war in Ukraine, and numerous other conflicts, such as the Sino-Japanese War, the Asia-Pacific War, the Korean War, and the Vietnam War. And the poet's sensitivity also encompasses the political and ethical fury toward this world of bad infinity.

4.

Then, at this juncture, we must acknowledge that we are facing radical problems and abandon our pessimistic outlook on them. How much longer will we continue to worship the myth of growth that sustains the world of bad infinity ("The End of Growth")? How much longer must we endure the "shame of being alive" ("The Final Stop"), contemplating our conformity to reality in the world of bad infinity where we "cannot return to the past" ("Outlook"), and "one small misstep, and [we] can't escape despair" ("Daydream"), in a world where we can only passively witness the "end of growth/Labor [being] legally exploited" ("Amplitude"), enthralled by the belief in surplus production of "excesses, energies that roam the earth" ("Mole"). At this rate, are we destined to accept "death without knowing anything" ("A New World") as the natural consequence within the logic of the world of bad infinity?

In response to this, poet Choi Ji-In, standing in front of the barricades, firmly proclaims a poetic resolution: "Those that make us feel/ ugly, foolish,/inadequate,/and hopeless//Unite/ In solidarity/If not, you will be plundered/and dominated/by those who consider you prey// Health/Food/Basic Income/Shelter Education//

We say to the warship/Get lost!"("Day and Night"). It is because the "solidarity of love" and the "love of solidarity" of the ones who do not remain silent in the world of bad infinity but actively struggle against it are the ways to profoundly and resolutely live out the life given us.

To love means
to live out

— Excerpt from "Day and Night"

PRAISE FOR CHOI JI-IN

K POET

When I heard that poet Choi Ji-In was working on a new poetry collection, I don't know the emotions he was experiencing. He loves labor, he loves love, and he is someone who works at accomplishing both without giving up either one. The problem is in that he is an artist—in my opinion, more of an artist than a poet. What's the difference between a poet and an artist? Oh, that's what you don't understand. You see, it's...

...

I see. But what's the problem with being an artist?

... You still don't get it.

At times Ji-in mistakes himself for a poet, a laborer, and a "loveist." Or perhaps he mistakenly envisions himself as an amalgamation of all three. I read many of his poems, heard about his labors, and remember the love he showed. But I don't believe that the sum of these is poet Choi Ji-In... I imagine the aspects of Choi Ji-In that I am unaware of—Choi Ji-In who cries unexpectedly while driving; Choi Ji-In who manages a smile to mask his sorrow; Choi Ji-In who flops down on the street on his way home to smoke a cigarette; Choi Ji-In who offers encouragement and solace to a friend even when he himself is feeling depressed...

Please keep in mind, these are solely my imaginations. But I do know that he is always persevering through challenges while trying not to show it.

How do I know this?

...That's not what piques my curiosity. Why doesn't Choi Ji-In talk about himself? It's because he is a fool. He gives love because he loves love, but he knows nothing about how to be loved. He is a fool. I'd once advised him not to try too hard. Yet foolish Choi Ji-In works too hard, and I know that he will continue to do so despite what I say to him. I feel as though he is a soldier trying to survive in the midst of war. I don't know what emotions he is experiencing. Because he is not a poet, a laborer, or a loveist—he is an artist.

Yang Anda (Poet)

K-POET
Am I Not Your Sin

Written by Choi Ji-In
Translated by Stella Kim
Published by ASIA Publishers
Address 445, Hoedong-gil, Paju-si, Gyeonggi-do, Korea
(Seoul Office:161-1, Seodal-ro, Dongjak-gu, Seoul, Korea)
Tel (822).3280.5058
Email bookasia@hanmail.net
Homepage Address www.bookasia.org

ISBN 979-11-5662-317-5 (set) | 979-11-5662-639-8 (04810)
First published in Korea by ASIA Publishers 2023

This book is published with the support of the Literature Translation Institute of Korea (LTI Korea).

K-픽션 시리즈 | Korean Fiction Series

〈K-픽션〉 시리즈는 한국문학의 젊은 상상력입니다. 최근 발표된 가장 우수하고 흥미로운 작품을 엄선하여 출간하는 〈K-픽션〉은 한국문학의 생생한 현장을 국내외 독자들과 실시간으로 공유하고자 기획되었습니다. 〈바이링궐 에디션 한국 대표 소설〉 시리즈를 통해 검증된 탁월한 번역진이 참여하여 원작의 재미와 품격을 최대한 살린 〈K-픽션〉 시리즈는 매 계절마다 새로운 작품을 선보입니다.

001 버핏과의 저녁 식사-**박민규** Dinner with Buffett-**Park Min-gyu**

002 아르판-**박형서** Arpan-**Park hyoung su**

003 애드벌룬-**손보미** Hot Air Balloon-**Son Bo-mi**

004 나의 클린트 이스트우드-**오한기** My Clint Eastwood-**Oh Han-ki**

005 이베리아의 전갈-**최민우** Dishonored-**Choi Min-woo**

006 양의 미래-**황정은** Kong's Garden-**Hwang Jung-eun**

007 대니-**윤이형** Danny-**Yun I-hyeong**

008 퇴근-**천명관** Homecoming-**Cheon Myeong-kwan**

009 옥화-**금희** Ok-hwa-**Geum Hee**

010 시차-**백수린** Time Difference-**Baik Sou linne**

011 올드 맨 리버-**이장욱** Old Man River-**Lee Jang-wook**

012 권순찬과 착한 사람들-**이기호** Kwon Sun-chan and Nice People-**Lee Ki-ho**

013 알바생 자르기-**장강명** Fired-**Chang Kang-myoung**

014 어디로 가고 싶으신가요-**김애란** Where Would You Like To Go?-**Kim Ae-ran**

015 세상에서 가장 비싼 소설-**김민정** The World's Most Expensive Novel-**Kim Min-jung**

016 체스의 모든 것-**김금희** Everything About Chess-**Kim Keum-hee**

017 할로윈-**정한아** Halloween-**Chung Han-ah**

018 그 여름-**최은영** The Summer-**Choi Eunyoung**

019 어느 피씨주의자의 종생기-**구병모** The Story of P.C.-**Gu Byeong-mo**

020 모르는 영역-**권여선** An Unknown Realm-**Kwon Yeo-sun**

021 4월의 눈-**손원평** April Snow-**Sohn Won-pyung**

022 서우-**강화길** Seo-u-**Kang Hwa-gil**

023 가출-**조남주** Run Away-**Cho Nam-joo**

024 연애의 감정학-**백영옥** How to Break Up Like a Winner-**Baek Young-ok**

025 창모-**우다영** Chang-mo-**Woo Da-young**

026 검은 방-**정지아** The Black Room-**Jeong Ji-a**

027 도쿄의 마야-**장류진** Maya in Tokyo-**Jang Ryu-jin**

028 홀리데이 홈-**편혜영** Holiday Home-**Pyun Hye-young**

029 해피 투게더-**서장원** Happy Together-**Seo Jang-won**

030 골드러시-**서수진** Gold Rush-**Seo Su-jin**

031 당신이 보고 싶어하는 세상-**장강명** The World You Want to See-**Chang Kang-myoung**

032 지난밤 내 꿈에-**정한아** Last Night, In My Dream-**Chung Han-ah**

Special 휴가중인 시체-**김중혁** Corpse on Vacation-**Kim Jung-hyuk**

Special 사파에서-**방현석** Love in Sa Pa-**Bang Hyeon-seok**